Concert and Contest COLLECTION

Compiled and Edited by H. VOXMAN

for ▶ Piano Accompaniment

TROMBONE with piano accompaniment

CONTENTS

Page Numbers

RUBANK®

HAL•LEONARD® CORPORATION
7777 W. BLUEMOUND RD. P.O. BOX 13819 MILWAUKEE, WI 53213

Après un Rêve
(After A Dream)

GABRIEL FAURÉ, Op. 7, No. 1
Transcribed by H. Voxman

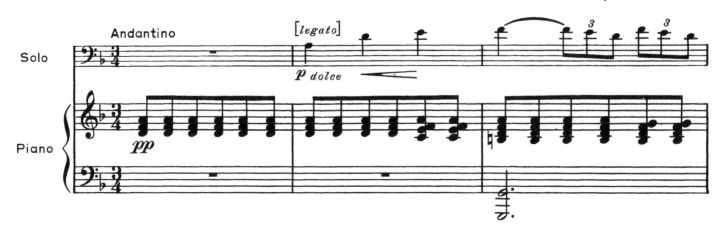

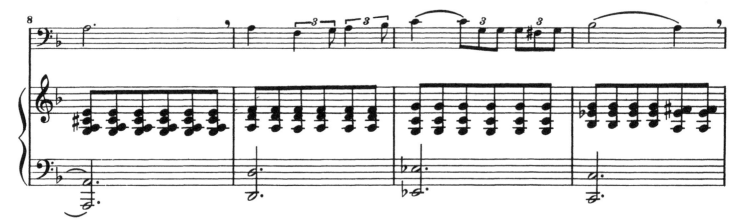

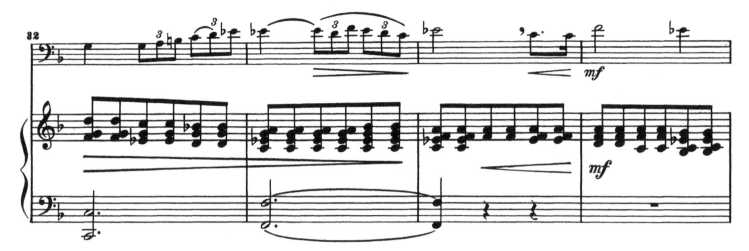

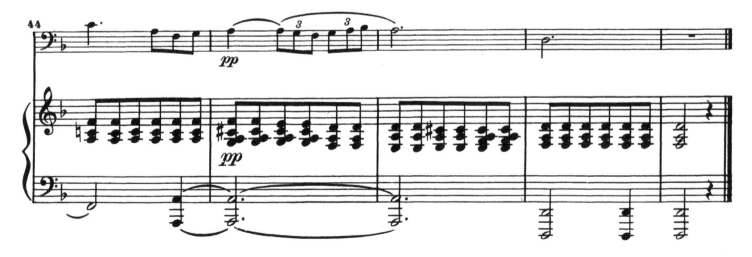

Valse Sentimentale

P. I. TSCHAIKOWSKY
Transcribed by H. Voxman

Canzonetta

W. A. MOZART
Adapted by H. Voxman

Two Spanish Dances

LEROY OSTRANSKY

I

II

13

Thème de Concours

ROBERT CLÉRISSE
Edited by H. Voxman

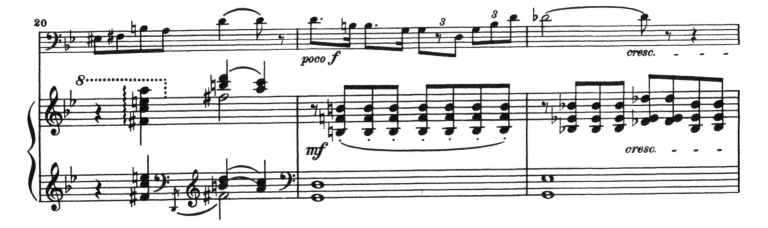

Sarabande and Vivace

G. F. HANDEL
Transcribed by H. Voxman

Love Thoughts

ARTHUR PRYOR
Transcribed by Clair W. Johnson

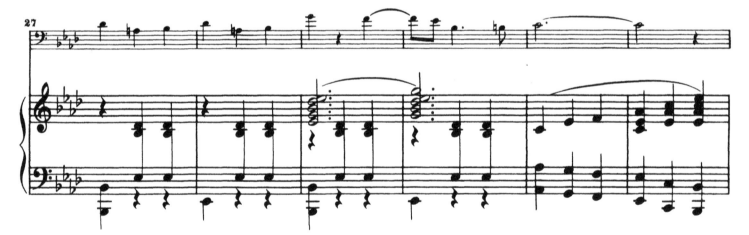

Legato

Morceau de Concours

EDMOND MISSA
Edited by H. Voxman

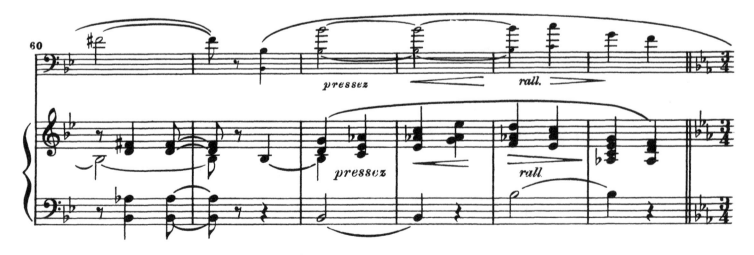

Crépuscule
(Twilight)

GABRIEL PARÈS
Edited by H. Voxman

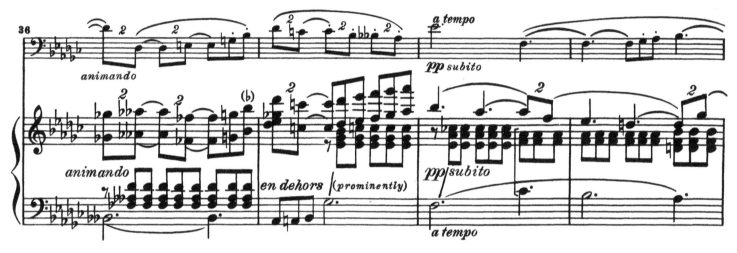

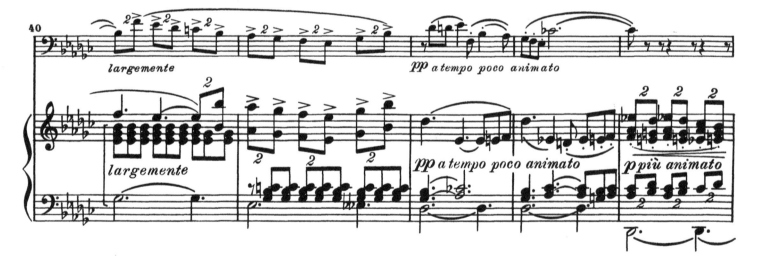

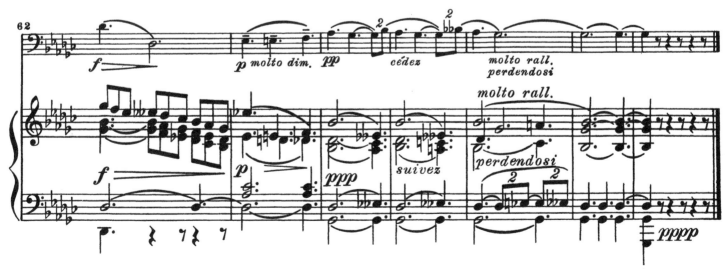

Concerto Miniature

LEROY OSTRANSKY

40

Andante con moto

43

Prelude and Fanfaronade

PAUL KOEPKE

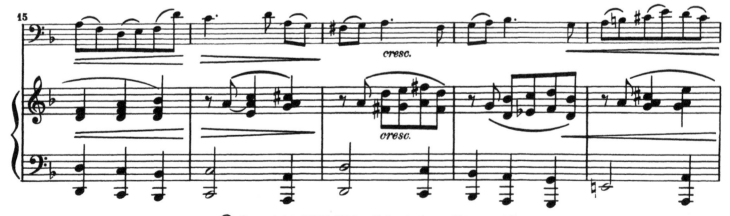

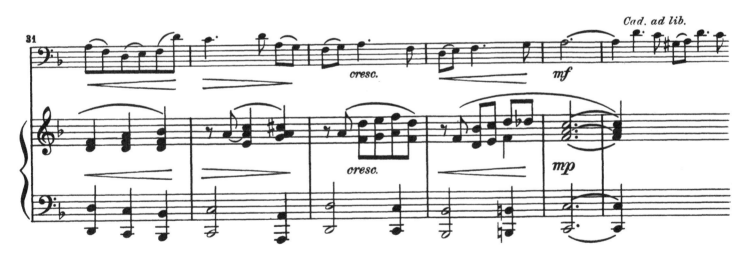

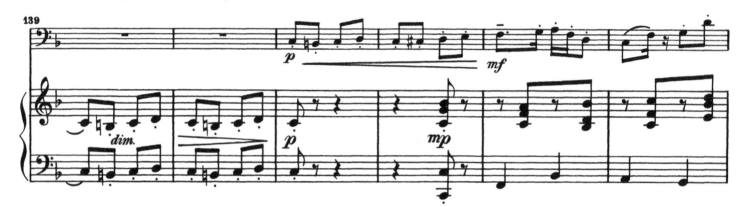

Solo de Concert

Th. DUBOIS
Edited by H. Voxman

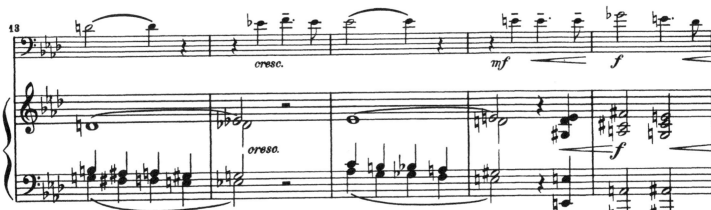

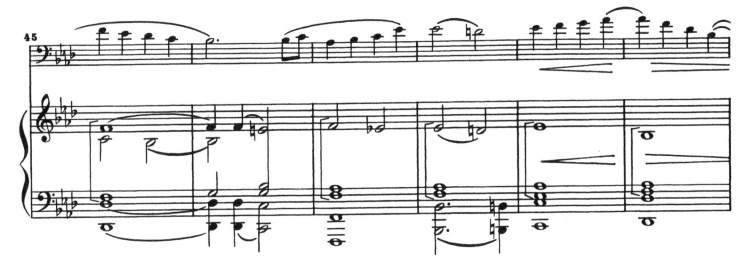

54

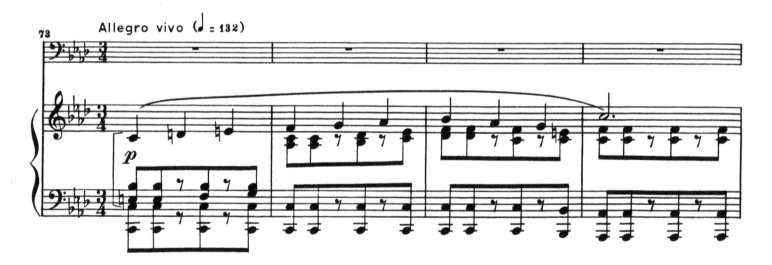

101
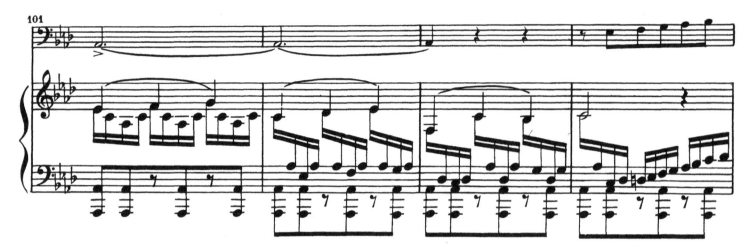

105
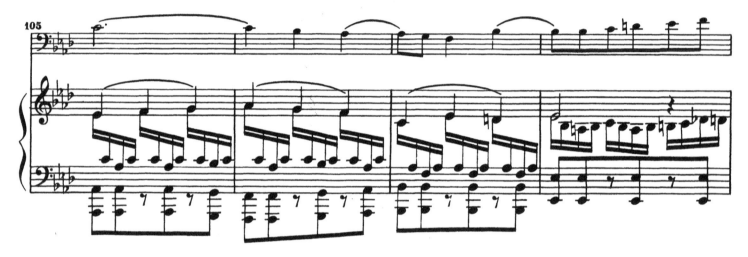

109

113

Concerto in F Minor

ÉMILE LAUGA
Edited by H. Voxman

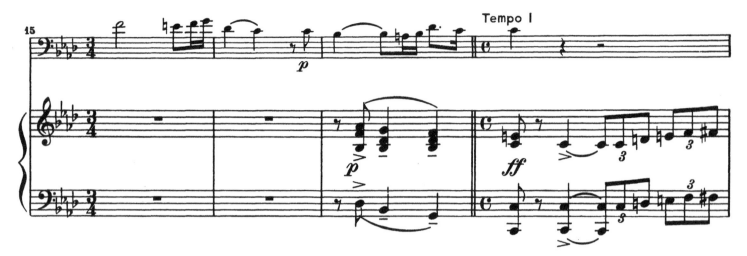

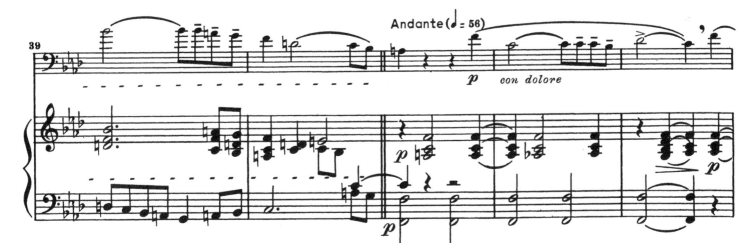

62

FINAL

66

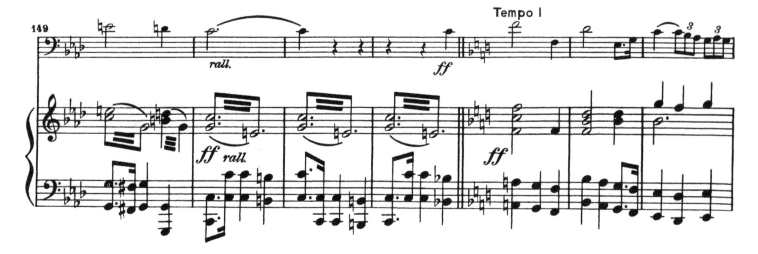

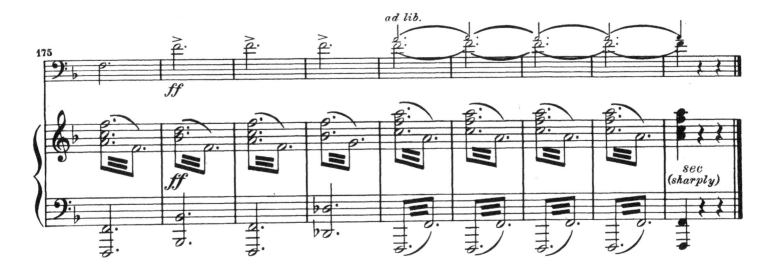

Allegro Vivace
from Concerto

Edited by H. Voxman

N. RIMSKY - KORSAKOFF
Arr. by N. Fedossejew

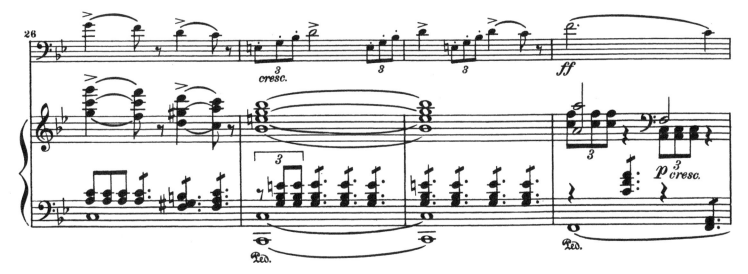